THE
PEOPLE'S CHOICE

*The Issues of the Campaign
as seen by the
Nation's Best Political Cartoonists*

Edited by Pierce G. Fredericks

DODD, MEAD & COMPANY • NEW YORK • 1956

FIRST...

The Peoples' Choice is an attempt to set out the issues of our present political campaign in one of journalism's oldest and most exciting forms — the political cartoon. There are about two hundred and seventy-five political cartoonists in the United States. They are working newsmen—most of them are expected to go to the drawing board and produce a witty, profound, perceptive cartoon at least five times a week.

In view of the heavy schedule, the quality of their work is extremely high. The diversity and vehemence of their opinions is one of the finest features of our press. They are obviously men of courage because a cartoon does not have the literary privilege of talking on both sides of a question—it has to come right out and say where it stands.

If it seems that the rebuke in cartooning is often delivered with more force than the pat on the back, it is because this is fundamentally an "agin'" medium. Its *forte* is blowing the whistle on those in power. Many a politician on gaining office has been grieved to find himself whomped by the very cartoonist who had been lambasting his predecessor.

Inevitably, someone's favorite cartoonist is left out of a book like this. I would particularly have liked to include some of the work of Herbert Block who signs himself Herblock, but his permission could not be obtained.

The presentation aims to be impartial. I have done my best and a member of the other major political party has gone over it with an eye to his side's interests.

PIERCE G. FREDERICKS

Green in The Providence Journal

Each four years we go through a presidential campaign and when it's over the winners and losers shake hands and exchange reasonably good wishes. This year as usual, though, plenty of dust will be raised, lots of brickbats will fly and some mud slung before the final handshakes. Most of the contention will be over the issues on the following pages.

Now the Republicans feel that no one will vote

against peace and prosperity.

Yoes in The San Diego Union

But Mr. Stevenson,

Senator Kefauver

White in The Akron Beacon-Journal

Mr. Truman

and Governor Harriman

Seibel in The Richmond Times-Dispatch

Little in The Nashville Tennessean

are eager to argue the point.

Hesse in The St. Louis Globe-Democrat

Long in The Minneapolis Tribune

Republicans say that the Democrats have no issues.

White in The Akron Beacon-Journal

Wood in The Richmond News Leader

Baldy in The Atlanta Constitution

To which the Democratic reply is "Is that so?"

AMERICA'S WORLD PRESTIGE

IKE'S BOLD DIPLOMACY

GENEVA

I*t is a major Republican claim that they have brought peace and improved foreign relations.*

Green in The Providence Journal

Democrats claim with equal vehemence that the accomplishments would have been impossible without Democrats like Senator George of Georgia.

Roche in The Buffalo Courier-Express

In Asia, Democrats say, the President has even been hindered by members of his own party like Senator Knowland.

Republican reply: we have the Asian situation well in hand.

Green in The Providence Journal

Pratt in The McClatchy Newspapers of California

Republican Secretary of State Dulles will be charged with confusing and frightening our allies with his statements.

Defenders, however, will picture Mr. Dulles as a sure-footed, farsighted, steady worker for peace.

Immel in The Peoria Journal

Fitzpatrick in The St. Louis Post-Dispatch

Hesse in The St. Louis Globe-Democrat

Neither party will deny that by and large we've been a prosperous country, but Democrats ask warily just where the boom is heading. Republicans call them "prophets of doom and gloom."

And while the administration will point with pride to

the soaring stock market . . .

Bimrose in The Portland Oregonian

. . . the opposition will ask what they have to say about the equally high-level cost of living.

Yardley in The Baltimore Sun

All politicians love farm states because there are so many of them. This year even the Republicans are willing to admit that there is some trouble down on the farm and that Secretary of Agriculture Benson is not perhaps the single most popular figure in the administration.

Crockett in The Washington Star

Little in The Nashville Tennessean

The Democrats have been asking just what sort of

farm program we have now . . .

. . . and Republicans reply that it's all very simple.

Pletcher in The Sioux City Journal

Manning from The McNaught Syndicate

Barrow in The Omaha World-Herald

Moreover, the Republicans
insist, if there is trouble,
it's all left over from
Democratic administrations.

Democrats, naturally,

Pratt in The McClatchy Newspapers of California

regard themselves as the only real friend the farmers have.

Secretary Benson feels that we'll all be happier
without rigid price supports.

Burck in The Chicago Sun-Times

There are those who differ with him, however,

and not all of them are Democrats.

A great many people admire Mr. Benson's

devotion to what he thinks is right...

. . . but very few of them would care to be in his shoes.

The Republicans said for years

that when they got into office there was going

Ficklen in The Dallas News

to be a big change in the way the taxpayers' money was handled.

Pletcher in The Sioux City Journal

Now, the Republicans are pointing to economy in government…

. . . and the Democrats are talking about the poor consumer.

G.O.P. BALANCED BUDGET

'56 SHOW

APOLOGIES TO EMMETT KELLY

Sandeson in The Fort Wayne News-Sentinel

The GOP presented the voters with a balanced budget this year

Fischetti—NEA Service

The Democrats, of course, have spent the past three years

reminding their rivals of this undelivered promise.

Ivey in The St. Petersburg Times

Little in The Nashville Tennessean

Unkind words are certain to be exchanged on tax cuts. One side will be accused of double talk...

. . . and the other of proposing tax cuts which couldn't possibly pass.

Crockett in The Washington Star

The Republicans will be charged with large talk and
small action on taxes . . .

Ficklen in The Dallas News

Yoes in The San Diego Union

. . . and the Democrats with having no regard for sound money.

Roche in The Buffalo Courier-Express

White in The Akron Beacon-Journal

There's going to be a special row over whether too little . . .

. . . or too much money is going to defense.

Crockett in The Washington Star

Fitzpatrick in The St. Louis Post-Dispatch

There are people in both parties who feel that we don't have enough Air Force . . .

Rosen in The Albany Times-Union

. . . and those who feel that, with atomic weapons, we have plenty.

Crawford in The Newark New[s]

It has been a long time since anything has divided Americans as badly as the security question.

Nobody's against security,

but we've had a hard time

agreeing on the details.

Pratt in The McClatchy Newspapers of California

Right wing Republicans haven't hesitated to charge that the Democrats were "soft on Communism."

Alexander in The Philadelphia Evening Bulletin

Immel in The Peoria Journal

And some even suggested that communists had practically taken over the government as a result.

More moderate people have begun to wonder if the investigators haven't been, at best, overenthusiastic ...

Justus in The Minneapolis Star

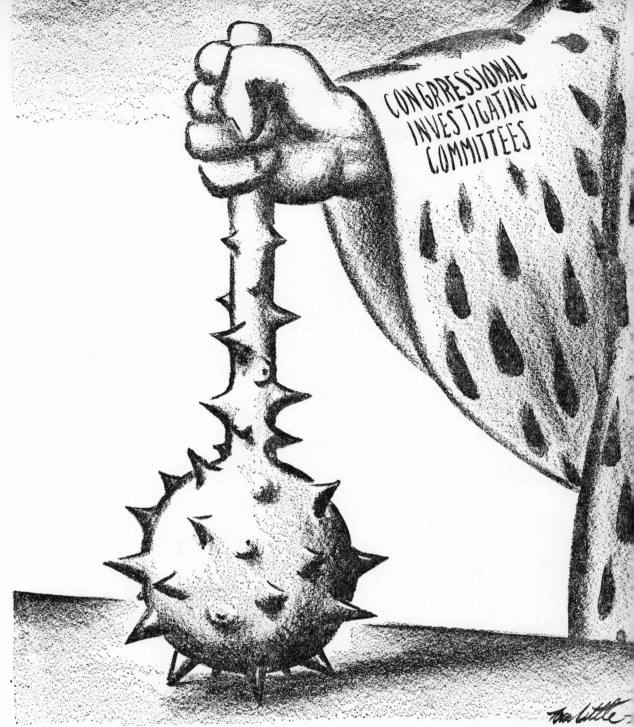

Little in The Nashville Tennessean

. . . and, at worst, sometimes less than fair.

Shanks in The Buffalo Evening News

Each side accuses the other of playing politics.

Republicans claim that the Democrats are frightened . . .

... and the Democrats return the compliment with emphasis

on Republican Attorney General Brownell.

While Republicans talk about the men they've let out
of government, Democrats will point to Secretary Benson
who fired Wolf Ladejinsky for security reasons
—only to see him cleared and reinstated.

Yoes in The San Diego Union

EZRA
TAFT
BENSON

LADEJINSKY

CASE

Fitzpatrick in The St. Louis Post-Dispatch

The Voice of America has been a favorite target of investigators.

Barrow in The Omaha World-Herald

Carmack in The Christian Science Monitor

The Voice's defenders have pointed out that it spent so much time under investigation that it had hardly any left to do its work.

The problem is still before the country: finding the best democratic

solution to the security question.

Shanks in The Buffalo Evening News

When we elected a Democratic Congress in 1954, everyone knew that there was scuffling ahead.

Crawford in The Newark News

Hesse in The St. Louis Globe-Democrat

HARMONY TALK

Republicans cry that Democrats have scuttled some of President Eisenhower's pet projects.

Fawcett in The Providence Evening Bulletin

Democrats reply that they've been a lot more help to

the President than his own party has.

Republicans will complain that the Democratic Congress didn't do the work it should have.

Yoes in The San Diego Union

Yardley in The Baltimore Sun

To which the Democrats will reply that there wouldn't have been any Eisenhower record except for Democratic votes.

G.O.P.

TIDELANDS SHADOW

York in The Louisville Courier-Journal

Who ought to have rights to what has been a running fight in this administration. The first big bone of contention was State vs. Federal control of our offshore oil deposits.

One side felt that oil under the ocean should be under Federal control

Pratt in The McClatchy Newspapers of California

Lewis in The Milwaukee Journal

The states-righters felt it belonged to the states nearest at hand.

Yoes in The San Diego Union

Wood in The Richmond News Leader

N

o sooner had the oil fight been resolved in favor of the states than a tussle began over public vs. private power.

Sandeson in The Fort Wayne News-Sentinel

Pratt in The McClatchy Newspapers of California

Democrats felt that Secretary McKay was too
partial to private power interests.

Republicans insisted that power was no business for the Federal government.

Hesse in The St. Louis Globe-Democrat

FEDERAL POWER

To which the Democrats replied "Give-away!"

Fitzpatrick in The St. Louis Post-Dispatch

Little in The Nashville Tennessean

Democrats feel that old projects like *TVA* will be curtailed and no new ones started.

Republicans insist that it's all part of a plan to get the government out of business it shouldn't be in anyway.

McCutcheon in The Spokane Spokesman-Review

Ray in The Kansas City Star

Wood in The Richmond News Leader

To Republicans, in fact, public power is a prime

example of "creeping Socialism."

Democrats are sure to counter with reminders of the Dixon-Yates private power contract which blew up into what Democrats call a scandal and Republicans call an unfortunate misunderstanding.

Pratt in The McClatchy Newspapers of California

The Dixon-Yates contract is dead now, but not for campaign purposes.

SENATOR SPARKMAN

SENATOR KEFAUVER

DEM. CHAIRMAN PAUL BUTLER

DIXON-YATES CONTROVERSY

DEMS.

Roche in The Buffalo Courier-Express

Seibel in The Richmond Times-Dispatch

The Democrats are going to have a lot to say about "businessman government" and the activities of some of the businessmen.

The Republican answer will be that businessmen are making a valuable contribution and that the bad apples have been thrown out of the barrel.

Sandeson in The Fort Wayne News-Sentinel

Pratt in The McClatchy Newspapers of California

There'll be plenty of firing from both sides over

whether the Salk vaccine program was well or badly handled.

Hesse in The St. Louis Globe-Democrat

E*ach side will accuse the other of being too hopelessly split to govern—the Republicans between left and right wings ...*

...and the Democrats between North and South.

Sandeson in The Fort Wayne News-Sentinel

Republicans have already accused the Democrats of
being labor dominated ...

. . . and have been told in return that they are the party of big business.

Little in The Nashville Tennessean

Republicans insist that they are not antilabor

. . . only antilabor-boss.

Barrow in The Omaha World-Herald

Poinier in The Detroit News

Democrats will remind them that the Taft-Hartley law

still stands and that the late Martin Durkin, Ike's

first Secretary of Labor, left the Cabinet in a huff.

Personalities in each party will collect their share of insults.
Republicans will dub Mr. Stevenson an egg-headed One Worlder...

. . . and Mr. Stevenson will undoubtedly survive and retaliate.

Vice-President Nixon, the Democrats' least favorite

Republican, will be denounced as a mud slinger...

Lewis in **The Milwaukee Journal**

Kuekes in The Cleveland Plain Dealer

...and the Republicans will defend him as a model Vice-President.

In other words, the Great '56 Campaign will be just as lively, noisy and bumptious as those before it. However...

Marcus in The New York Times

... to well-wishers abroad, who sometimes fear for us during these family disputes, and to ill-wishers abroad, who hope it'll get worse, a word based on experience: when it's all over, the Republic will once more have survived, and very nicely, thank you.

DATE DUE

MAR 1 - 1976

MAY 30 1977

FEB 15 1994